The View From Windows to the Soul

Toni Johnson

BookLeaf Publishing

India | USA | UK

Presentation by *BookLeaf Publishing*

Web: www.bookleafpub.com

E-mail: info@bookleafpub.com

ISBN: 9789357691765

First edition 2022

DEDICATION

My Mother & Her Mother, RIP. I am
everchanged. One of many for you both.

I. Trip

When I opened my windows today, things didn't feel like they had the previous day. Sun rays no longer burned my eyes, the same way, I could gaze into its eternal light undisturbed by its bright. My lungs have opened to taste the sweetness in the air. Each molecule performing its own ballet on my taste buds renewed senses, improved vision, even the skin I live in feels different. No longer the perfect fit I was born with, I've outgrown it. Entire body tingling, like my entire body's been sleeping. Opening the windows today, I am awake. Auto pilot disabled, and the next move is on me to choose. I opened my windows today, a new.

II. No good in good mourning

Morning. Good morning. In mourning. Once upon a Time, sunshine meant a good morning. Blue skies in the morning were heartwarming. Blue skies in mourning leave yearning. At one point, sunrise filled me with hope for the day. Now each sunrise reminds me of the pain that you're gone from me yet another day. Mourning will never be the same. Maybe, I'll sleep forever, where it will always be night.

III. It's all sunken from here

I'm definitely in a sunken place, devoid of
sound, and other people, and I think I want to
stay. Stirring circles in my coffee mug, falling
deeper than graves are dug. The light gradually
slips away, now I'm grasping at darkness, while
engulfed in disarray. I know my coffee is too
sweet when my thoughts get this deep but I just
keep stirring up emotions that lead me to weep.
Something of a masochist, I relish in the pain. I
dig my fingers in the bruises and temporarily I
feel sane. Although really, there's nothing sane
about it, I'm not ashamed about it, though my
brain may be clouded, may be deranged.
Honestly, I don't doubt it. In the sunken place, I
don't need to explain why I'm this way. In the
infinite bleak, I can unzip me, remove this
earthly flesh, and obey the demand to portray
my true self.

IV. Misplaced Ending

I might close the door today. And I mean that in more ways than I can clearly say. I might choose to ignore today and the day before and anymore that may prove to add to my disarray. I may flip the switch on my sanity and humanity cause I'd rather be free from the agony that shatters me. I might choose to end it, not life but the strife that exists in it. Just don't have the fight anymore, I can't win it. I might disappear, never felt at home here anyway. This might be the day it just all goes away. At least I can say that I've tried, even in spite of my cries. I still tried to smile.

V. Now What

My heart is full and open,
My brain full of commotion.
Just trying to get the two
operating on the same notion.

The notion that there's
no need to fear.
Fear the feelings that
are now here,
Against my better judgement;
Against my will.
They are here and they are real.

The notion that I can do it all again.
Although I said the last
one was the end.
I said "I will never commit"
Trauma response saying
I don't have the strength within.

Strength to give me
to another human being.
And trust that he and we
will not, figuratively,
abuse the other.
Neither emotionally

or mentally.

So now what do I do?
Now that I love you…
The universe said
"Fuck your plans!"
They say focusing on
what you don't want;
will make precisely that
come true.

So while I said, I want
nothing new, not trying
to pursue anything that
involves mi corazon.
I got precisely that which
I wanted to leave alone.
My plans got overthrown.
And I can't postpone what
my heart condones.

So what new; now what?
Feel the full spectrum &
trust, that there's still
enough.

There's still enough love,
Inside me existing to
give another.

VI. Expect The Unexpected

Resistance is futile.
You couldn't resist if you tried to.
You've learned not to oppose the way things
come, or go.
No one ever knows when their person is going to
show, but when they do, you know you don't say
no.
Non-resistance is allowing life to flow.
We may never truly know, reasons for seasons,
but it's undeniable that we really do need them.
With gratitude, you accept new love.
Before you convince yourself, you're
undeserving because of wrongs you had done.
If it finds you, while you're trying to, deny you'll
ever love, it's divine proof of what the heart is
capable of.
The power of a heart that finds you in darkness,
shining light on your most neglected, emotional
compartments.
A spark ignites to a twin flame, what's really in
that name anyway, but this heart is the fire,
burning, passionate and untamed, when
combined with your air, both wild and
unashamed to proclaim that you are truly in love
for the last time. Again.

VII. What is a Twin Flame?

What is a twin flame?
Is it but a name that implies we, two, are the
same at the soul?
Kindred spirits with a mutual goal to become
whole with each other.
Meanwhile, we encounter lovers who's intent is
to smother that burning flame.
It's purpose to shine bright and act as a guiding
light for our destinies to ignite with one another
again, because it feels like I've known you in a
past life.
And oddly, things feel so familiar, effortless
comfort and connection seems so peculiar.
What is this phenomenon that only happens once
upon, a life time?
On that we can agree, that very rarely do we
stumble on, a person so destined to be, likely,
just like you.
Hence the word twin being used to infuse the
sentiment that you two reciprocate the same
views.
That your vibes effortlessly fuse, like paper does
to glue, like the sky does to blue.
Everything so smooth and nonresistant, Free to
be yourself with them so why resist it?

You don't, you go with the flow because you
must know there can be no repetition of
something so exquisite.
But what is it?
What is a twin flame?

VIII. My Piece

Lately, feeling unmotivated
has got me slightly frustrated.
Still grieving so I also stay sedated.
When my mind is elevated,
prose is easily orchestrated.
Words flow uncontrolled and unabated.
So much that, I feel at ease to say this
I have found peace with you.
With you, I'm more elated
than if I were on shrooms.
Somehow, you inspire me to,
actually do, everything I mean to.
And really things I need to be
doing anyway.
If ever I am lost for words to say,
you have a way that motivates
my tangled mental state, to be
restful and to create. Everyday.
Shown I can trust what you say
so like a good girl, I obey.
Now as of late, I pray you'll stay,
At my side, My peace.

IX. Kiss Me

I will admit I am impressed and more or less obsessed, by the lips you are blessed to possess. And now my thoughts would suggest, unrest until I am acquiesced with the privilege to test their tenderness. Imagining their warmth and how they must feel, causes me to reel. It's unreal…how they steal my attention. So much that, I can't conceal my intention, to seal the deal with the intervention of my own. I meticulously observe each infinitesimal gesture and your tone, as your words escape their home behind an oral throne. I can't suppress the desire to condone their gentle placement, both on my face and below my waist then, every space in between. I voluntarily relinquish control and allow your lips to make me whole and full of everything you choose to bestow. I imagine my knees will weaken and my portal leaking at every single meeting of our lips. It's perplexing that a mere kiss could cause me to drip below the hips like this but there is nothing "mere" at all about what sits so tactfully placed upon your face. Truthfully, I expect that I'll experience no less than sheer bliss when I finally get to kiss your lips.

X. Surrender

Something happens nightly;
Where these thoughts creep in impliedly.
They're inappropriate, don't mind me,
but also blatantly enticing.
Vividly outlined in my mind, visions of your
physique and mine, intertwined.
Vibing between sheets as your fingers trace all
over me.
Sending tremors from my head down to my feet.
As we lay and our lips meet, immense heat rises
in between our bodies as well as between my
thighs and I can't hide the excitement incited in
my privates.
This sudden surge of fluids means we like it.
And the mouth might try but the body can't deny
it.
So instead I surrender, your mouth takes me
prisoner, trying to put me at ease by working
towards my release.
Sincerely affirming, I've been a good girl and I
deserve it.
And I confirm this without words but with
oceans and torrent.

And after you've made me, your personal siren of the sea, it's my turn to devour that which now belongs to me.

XI. Chemistry

Your essence is encapsulated in the infinite spaces of my subconscious. However, consciously as well, your presence exists as a promise to return, repeatedly. Although fleetingly, as I remind myself, you are not mine, but free to be, whatever you incline. And while I imply that I'm fine with whatever you decide, inside, I hope that your mind craves me as frequently as I beseech thee. Striving to appear unbothered and ever cool, truthfully, I'm awkward, and being ruled by overwhelming desire to share skin with you. By that, I simply mean closeness, not to be confused with the motions, we create, if we laid beside each other, trading fluids under covers. But yes, please, that too. You have formulated tidal waves inside me, by naturally arising, thought that revives me. A side of me I had been hiding, to not seem high and mighty. Watered down my true identity but here you've come to find me. As if I've been here, the same person, all along, dormant, missing some thing that has always belonged. A part of me, and like some kind of king charming or high-quality gentleman of class, you've awakened me, to be who I should've been, and who I must be at last.

XII. Hello There

You see me.
The side of me buried under conformity.
For survival but you see the real me.
The me I hide from a close-minded society.
You see my obscurity and remind me of its
beauty.
You see straight through me to the celestial
being beneath.
I can look back at you unafraid because in your
eyes, I feel safe.
You see me, so I exist naturally. Emphatically.
I am me, a rarity, on this planet solely to spare
humanity from its damning.
Somehow, you see that and don't retract your
infatuation.
In your own way, you are the same, that explains
the acceptation.
With you, I am at an ease that feels like summer
breezes with sweet tea.
Swinging in a hammock under palm trees.
Probably on a beach, if I list all the things that
soothe me.
As if you always knew me, it's lucid, yet
conducive, to be seen.

XIII. Gold Caps & Green Lady

As my soul escapes me down a rabbit hole, into the wonderland that is my imagination, I inhale, taking her back deep inside to the hollows, unexplored. Dark and cold, and sometimes cruel. She fills me…to an explosion in my subconscious, thought provoking trauma to my insides, but I like it. I crave this…bound by addiction to vision, she weakens the fire inside me. She enlightens me… Green lady, purple third eye.

XIV. Balance Out The Lows

It's Friday.
Just as good a day as any to get high day.
Trying to combat the things that I feel is too hard
anyway.
Always searching for an escape.
Anything that will take me away.
It's only Friday but I'll return everyday.
I no longer have the strength to dwell in this
plane where people talk to my face but my focus
is misplaced.
The only time I can align is when I'm high.
Out of my mind, not all there, denying the
despair that's inside but it's there.

XV. Endless Tears of a Clown

They say crying is good for you;
so now the tears won't stop.
Apparently, I need a lot of what's good for me.
And until I've had my fill, I'll have my feel of
endless tears.
Hopefully, at some point, I'll be good enough
that they can stop.
Sad or not, tracks of my tears linger behind.

XVI. Culpe Os Cogumelos

One evening, I heard the sky speak.
Eyes of burning stars, gazed upon me with
familiarity.
It was chilly but a warmth succumbed me.
Clouds parted ways politely, nothing present to
intervene.
A voice, robust and transcendent, reverberated
internally.
Commanding my movements, "surrender
control" it tells me.
Unwillingly, I collapse to my knees.
The sky proceeds to read me, tell me all the
things impeding my acsending, mentally.
It tells me the ego is lying when I think I'm
already enlightened, divinely.
Reminds me there's still so much that's inciting
to my psyche and not to go on blindly, thinking I
know enough to guide me or anybody through
life.
All I could do was agree, while on my knees,
tears of humility streamed down my cheeks.
Understanding had been reached.
It's one thing to hear the sky speak,
it's another to be listening.

XVII. Say It Like You Mean It

It's unexpected, it's sudden, but I'm receptive.
I say it's soon, it's early, it's fast but time is
constraint made by man.
Who says what I feel is not real simply because
it's timing doesn't appeal with the ideal that
humans have conceived?
Who says what they believe is correct?How can
anyone object when souls naturally connect?
Especially because humans are flawed, how can
they claim to know anything at all?
Who says they're right?
My heart says overwrite their spite, ignore their
abhor, feel this love with all your might.
Ignore their deterrent to anything divergent, trust
your discernment.
If you feel it's worth it, nevermind their concern
with, matters of your heart because no one on
earth has part in what you do, this is between
just you two, and what could be more solid and
more real than what both of you feel.
When it's mutual, it's beautiful, it's irrefutable.
So time and things made up by man, can kiss my
ass!

When I say I love you I mean that no cap, no gas, just facts.

XVIII. I'm trying, Mom

Naturally, gravity grapples me, plummets me
savagely, back to reality.
No time to dwell on what saddens me, I have to
be a beacon of clarity.
'Cause these three little people rely on regularity,
can't afford to be narrowly hanging on, barely,
being strong. Carefully moving toward a state of
moving forward.
To a place that's in accord with a heart and mind
in sync.
To a place where I can think….clearly, I'm on
the brink of being nearly extinct.
Cause all that is me, is basically obsolete.
Those that created me, gone in a blink, of an
eye.
Here today, gone by tonight. Taken from me by
a thief, in the night, don't cry.
And even when you lie, some will still see, the
sadness you bleed.

XIX. Wicked

The crazy thing is people are addicted to this
sick shit.
The twisted reality that you've gotta get lifted to
exist in.
My mind drifted for a minute, thinking about
riffs in time, when this kid on the curbside
might've had a better life.
Where he wasn't always high, posted up with a
sign, tryna get by or some coke for a line. You
never know…but whatever his vice, one thing I
know is, it's wicked.
Dismiss it, avert our eyes like we missed it, we
didn't.
He even waved, we winced at it.
His sign said "everybody needs help" even the
addict.
And maybe we grimaced but that shit was felt.
Even under the influence of crack, he still had
truth to tell.
It's wicked how we kick it like rocks ain't
addictive. We kick it like we've figured it all out
& now we're above this.
You're just addicted to the best shit, that
deception.

Where you've got zero recollection of the real
shit you just stepped in & now you're tracking it
in every direction.
Spread it till it's popularity rises like erections.
And it's ironic that they're both hard, hard to
disconnect with.
Justify it as a necessary obsession, the fact we
think we're any different than this kid, it's
wicked.

XX. Word To The Wise

I can be fleeting.
I can be quick and I can slip from your grip if
you don't hang tight to it.
My heart that is.
I can be convinced that no feelings exist and
then I'll drift and I'll forget.
So always remind me, daily and nightly.
Hold me tightly, kiss me and delight me.
I don't want to lose what I currently feel for you,
and given too much room, that's exactly what
I'll do.
I can get bored, if my desires are ignored.
So give me more, even than I'm asking for.
I deserve it, I'm worth it.
I'll return it, unconditional, love galore.
I have that here for you, if you're committed and
loyal.
Hold tightly to my heart so our love won't soil.

XXI. Tiffany

Did you know?
All of me would go with you when you go.
Did you know?
Losing you would take such a toll.
I don't know, mommy, how to keep going but
I'm trying.
'Cause I think it's what you'd want me to do.
There's no price on what I'd pay to call you, your
voice is my favorite tune but suddenly I've gone
mute.
Have you stopped hearing me too?!
When I cry at night because I can't hug you.
Can you still hear me say I love you?
My everything since you gave me life.
Mommy, where did you go?
There was so much fight in the woman I know.
Feeling robbed of my best friend, now another
Angel.
Please tell my Daddy that I said hello.
Can't pass the stage of accepting it's real.
For as long as I live, nothing will change how I
feel.
Not love, not money, not trips overseas…
Nothing in the world can replace you to me.

Tiffany…there are things I'll probably always blame myself for, as if they could have changed things…
I just pray that you forgive me and that you're resting in peace, Mommy.